The earliest known painting of Berkeley Castle

Many things have been writte
the imaginative interpretation

Seen from the meadows it
hewn out of natural rock. No
to herself the masses of stone reared seven-and-a-half centuries
ago. The giant walls and mighty buttresses look as if they have
been carved by wind and weather out of some solid rock-mass,
rather than wrought by human handiwork.

When the day is coming to its close, and the light becomes a
little dim, and thin mist-films arise from the meadows, it might be
an enchanted castle, for in some tricks of evening light it cheats
the eye into something ethereal, without substance, built up for the
moment into towering masses of pearly vapour.

It is indeed an enchanted castle, in spite of its massive solidity. It has also been written of Berkeley that it has a swagger of its own.

I can see no reason to revise these words.

Berkeley is indeed swagger, and it is also beautiful in its rough uncouth way. People whose taste inclines to neat Queen Anne or Georgian houses will not care for Berkeley: it is neither cosy nor manageable. It is alarming. It exacts a high level of living from the soul. You cannot begin to understand Berkeley if all that you desire is comfort, security, and nice small warm convenient rooms. Berkeley is not like that. It is savage, and old, and unique.

Right:
Mr. and Mrs. R.J.G. Berkeley
with their two sons

1

The Outer
Courtyard and
West Front

INTRODUCTION

*I*n the charter granted to Robert
FitzHarding by Henry II, Henry
covenants to build up a castle himself,
secundum voluntatem ipsius Roberti,
which we could translate to mean
according to the said Robert's wishes.

The 14th century door within
the Norman portal

whether King Henry or FitzHarding bore the cost of the work is not known, but what seems clear is that the Keep dates from 1117, the date of the Charter. It is of the type known as a shell-keep, and is of special interest in that it surrounds the whole of the original mound, instead of following the usual practice of being perched on top of it.

Main Entrance to the Castle from the Inner Bailey

The Inner Courtyard

THE KING'S GALLERY

Up a flight of steps is the room which possibly contains Berkeley's most dramatic story – the imprisonment and eventual murder of King Edward II. But today it contains a fine collection of paintings depicting members of the Royal family. A notable item of furniture is the Cypress chest which once belonged to Sir Francis Drake.

Left: Queen Elizabeth of Bohemia, Paul van Somers

Right: Prince Henry, son of James I English School 17th century

In the far left corner of the room is a circular hole in the floor surrounded by a wooden rail. This was the Dungeon and goes down 28 feet to the level of the Courtyard. Rotting carcasses of cattle and other animals would be thrown down into the pit so the appalling smell could rise up and eventually asphyxiate the poor prisoner in the room above.

If the captive was of lowly birth, he would be thrown down on top of the carcasses to rot with them in the charnel-well.

Mary of Modena, 2nd wife of King James II by Sir Peter Lely

Edward's constitution must have been strong, because the fumes and incarceration did not end his life as intended. In the end he was murdered in his bed by his jailors, Sir John Maltravers and Sir Thomas Gurney. What part in the events Thomas Lord Berkeley took is not clear. All we do know is that he was not in residence during the King's captivity.

George I

KING EDWARD'S ROOM

*King Edward's
seal*

The shrieks of death through Berkeley's roof that ring,

Shrieks of an agonizing King

KING EDWARD II
MARLOWE

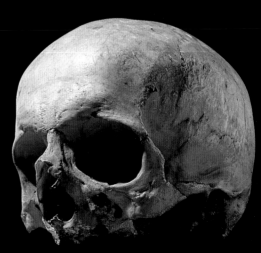

Drake's Room with the portrait of Christine Lady Berkeley, wife of John, the first Lord Berkeley by Sir Peter Lely

DRAKE'S ROOM
&
TOWER ROOM

*Jane, Lady Berkeley of Stratton
by Sir Peter Lely*

O n the right of the King's Gallery is a door to what is known as Sir Francis Drake's Bedroom. It contains a

The carved oak bedhead

beautifully carved oak four-poster bed and a fine pair of portraits of John and Jane Berkeley by Sir Peter Lely.

8

*John, Lord Berkeley of Stratton
by Sir Peter Lely*

Through a narrow door and passage which cuts through the thickness of the Keep, is the Tower Room. This contains an unusual collection of mid–17th century ebony furniture, which, so the tradition says, once belonged to Sir Francis Drake. It came into this country from the Portuguese East Indies under the influence of Queen Catherine of Braganza, the Portuguese wife of King Charles II.

The furniture is beautifully carved; the back of this chair incorporates ivory within its design of native people and animals of India

*Classic Chippendale
style frame*

THE PICTURE GALLERY

own a short flight of steps is the Picture Gallery. The sea-pieces are of special interest as most of the ships illustrated were commanded by members of the Berkeley family. If you look closely you can see their coats of arms on the sterns of the vessels.

There are some good Dutch and English paintings and marquetry tables and furniture of the late seventeenth century. The wooden model in the centre is a fine example of an Admiralty model used when constructing warships.

Newmarket racecourse in the reign of George I by the Dutch artist Peter Tillemans

Berkeley and its Castle in the 17th century by Henry Dankerts

Groom and Horses by George Stubbs

Below:
Old Berkeley Hounds findin' Bricket Wood circa
1820, ascribed to Ben Marshall

Above:
A detail from William Van de Velde's seascape
'The Tyger'; the painting's inscription reads:
'The TYGER commanded by CHARLES Lord
BERKELEY of STRATTON in the year 1681
and who died on board that ship in 1682. The
portrait of him is by Sir Peter Lely.

THE DINING ROOM

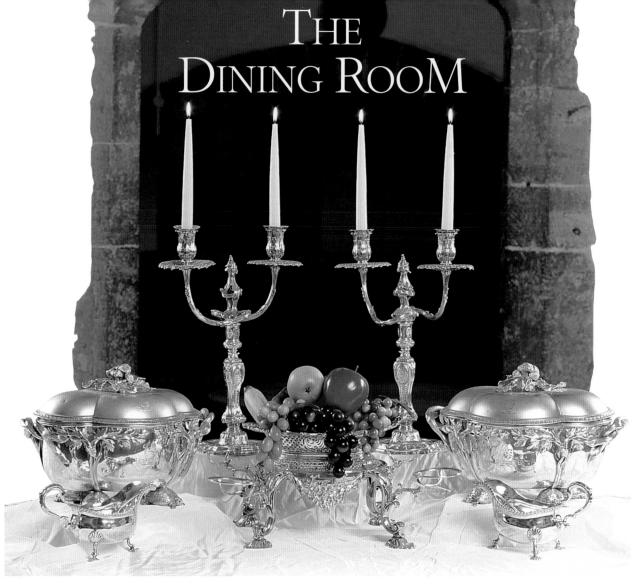

Pieces from the 18th century Dining Room silver service

Via a staircase housing portraits of the 19th century Lords Fitzhardinge, you reach the Billiard Room, now displayed as the Dining Room. Although it was not originally designed as such, it is the perfect space to display the large late 18th century dining table and accompanying furniture. On the walls is a collection of Berkeley portraits, with one particularly interesting example being the portrait of Sir William Berkeley who became Governor of Virginia in America in 1641.

Mahogany wine cooler and knife boxes

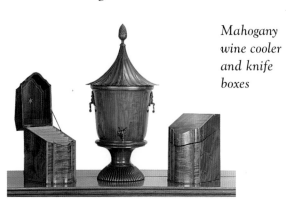

Capt. R.G. Berkeley by Raoul Millais

Charles 3rd Baron
FitzHardinge by
William Edward
Miller

Mr R.J.G.
Berkeley by
J.M. Teesdale

The 8th Earl of
Berkeley by Sir
William Orpen

13

Cooking utensils and below:
the kitchen range and rotating spit

Dr. Edward Jenner (the discoverer of the
vaccination against smallpox)
attributed to James Sharples

THE GAME LARDER, BUTTERY & KITCHEN

The only access to the other side of the Castle is through a number of small office rooms, dairies and game larders. These comparitively dull rooms have been decorated with paintings and objects of interest.

The medieval Buttery and Kitchen date from the 14th century and are very little altered. In their day they would have been the fulcrum for all life at the Castle. In the Buttery the sinks, pestle and mortar, chopping blocks and other kitchen utensils have all been retained. The arches on the walls show the positions of the early bread ovens. In the kitchen the old grate with a large series of spits is of interest, as is the whole arrangement of this fourteenth century kitchen with its several fireplaces. Particularly interesting survivals are the Tudor timbered roof and the sinks of solid lead. Underneath the Buttery is a subterranean passage which leads to the main well of the Castle, situated underneath the Courtyard. Until fairly recently this well provided water, not only for the Castle, but for the whole town.

The Buttery

THE CHINA RooM

As its name suggests, this room contains cabinets displaying a fine collection of Worcester, Wedgwood and other services. In many cases these are decorated with the arms of the Berkeley family. In a perspex frame opposite is an embroidered bedspread said to have been owned by Queen Elizabeth I and used during her visits to Berkeley. In the window is a case containing some Elizabethan embroidered cushions of the same series.

Chamberlain Worcester Presentation Vase

Chamberlain Worcester Ice Pail

Derby Sauce Tureen

Worcester Sauce Tureen

Queen Elizabeth's bedspread in the China Room

THE HOUSEKEEPER'S ROOM

The Housekeeper's Room is the repository for a collection of late 18th century furniture and several interesting pictures, including a winter scene by Ruisdael. Shown in a grille in the wall is the Godwin Cup, by tradition said to have belonged to Earl Godwin, father of King Harold.

A low stone medieval door leads from this room into the Screens from where a dramatic view of the Great Hall is obtained.

The famous Godwin cup

THE GREAT HALL

This magnificent Hall measuring 32½ feet high, 62 feet long and 32 feet wide, is of the 14th century, built within the 12th century curtain wall of the Castle which may be seen on the left where it has been pierced for two window openings. The Great Hall was built on the site of the original in the reign of King Edward III *c.* 1340 by Thomas, 3rd Lord Berkeley. The roof dates from the same period, but there is a historical record that it was repaired extensively in 1497 when it is possible that the upper part was lowered to the present saddle-topped style. The walls are hung with a fine series of Oudenarde tapestries illustrating the History of Queen Esther.

Lord Hunsdon by Mark Gerards
Grandfather of Elizabeth m. Sir Thomas Berkeley

Carved door bearing the Berkeley arms

The stained glass in the windows, showing the various alliances of the family, was set up between the two World Wars.

The 16th century Screen at the end of the Hall should be noted for it retains its original painted decoration, though the painting of the charges on the shields has been changed. The pictures above the tapestries are of various members of the family. Above the fireplace is a portrait of Admiral Sir George Cranfield Berkeley by Gainsborough. From the dais of the Hall great doors open onto the Grand Staircase. Notice the well-preserved example of the 'Berkeley Arch'.

Left: detail of George 1st Earl of Berkeley by Mary Beale

BERKELEY CHAIRS

There are chairs of many styles and periods in the Castle. Here are some of them with an indication of the rooms in which they can usually be found.

Black-painted beechwood armchair, late 17th century – The Morning Room

Mahogany ladder-back chair – The Dining Room

Chinese chair, Charles II – The Picture Gallery

Oak armchair, early 17th century – The Great Hall

Walnut chair by Daniel Morot – The Grand Stairs

Oak armchair, early 17th century – The Great Hall

Gilt side-chair, George I – The Long Drawing Room

Regency armchair – The Dining Room

Walnut frame armchair, early 18th century – The King's Gallery

Hepplewhite mahogany shield-back armchair – The Housekeeper's Room

The Great Hall

The Screen in the Great Hall

*Right: Admiral Sir George
Cranfield Berkeley by
Gainsborough*

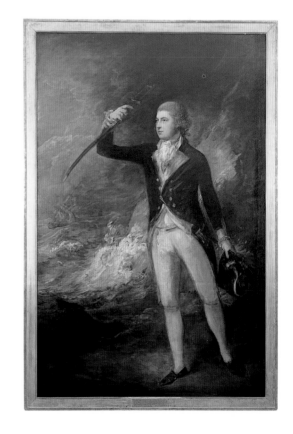

*The top of the 16th century Italian
walnut pedestal stand*

THE GRAND STAIRS

This fine wooden staircase dates from 1637. On the landing are four fine hoop-back Queen Anne chairs with their embroidered seats, and a Chinese lacquer cabinet. On the walls are some examples of late 16th century embroidery formerly part of the hangings of a bed-chamber in the Castle. A portrait between the doors is a contemporary copy by Old Stone of a Self Portrait of Van Dyck and here are also a portrait by Francis Cotes of Admiral Sir George Cranfield Berkeley as a Midshipman, and one by Reynolds of Elizabeth Drax, who embroidered the suite of furniture to be seen in the Long Drawing Room.

Nell Gwynne by Sir Godfrey Kneller

21

THE MORNING ROOM

At one time the Chapel of St. Mary, the Morning Room is interesting mainly for its timber roof with contemporary painted decoration, chiefly in reds and greens somewhat restored, and containing verses from an early translation of the Revelation of St. John the Divine. The translation was made by John Trevisa, one of the chaplains of the Castle, in 1387. The translation is from Latin to Norman French and is interesting not only for its decorative value but because it is part of one of the earliest attempts to render the Scriptures into the language of the Englishman of the time. John Trevisa, a Cornishman, was born about 1342 and came to Berkeley about 1380. He was a friend of Wycliffe, with whose views he was in complete sympathy. He died at the age of 60 and is buried in the chancel of Berkeley Church.

In the Morning Room is a magnificent series of early Brussels tapestries, depicting the story of Isaac and Rebecca, and Sodom and Gomorrah, woven by the Pannemakers after cartoons by Raphael. The very fine refectory table traditionally came from Fountains Hall.

Part of the stone carving on the medieval chimneypiece

A section of the timber
roof showing verses from
John Trevisa's translation
of the Revelation of St.
John the Divine

THE LONG DRAWING ROOM

One of the main features of this splendid room is the superb series of carved gilt wall mirrors, two of which incorporate the Berkeley Arms in the cresting.

Accompanying these is a suite of carved giltwood furniture
all embroidered in petit-point by Elizabeth Drax, the wife
of the 4th Earl. The carpet is a Hispano-Moresque. At the
end of the room is the King's Pew, formerly in the Chapel.

*Mrs. John Berkeley
by John Redvers*

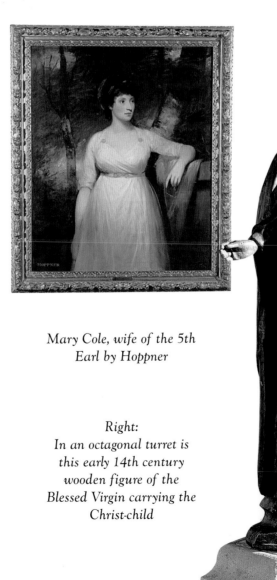

*Mary Cole, wife of the 5th
Earl by Hoppner*

*Right:
In an octagonal turret is
this early 14th century
wooden figure of the
Blessed Virgin carrying the
Christ-child*

25

THE SMALL DRAWING ROOM

One of the items in the cabinet

Gilt furniture and another series of fine Brussels tapestries help to make this a charming room, soft and mellow in colour and very suitable for its purpose as an evening room.

In the cabinet in the corner is an attractive collection of objects in soapstone, ivory, jade, amber and bronze. The tapestries, the subjects of which are taken from Ovid's Metamorphoses, bear the name of their weaver, Jan Cobus, and the Arms above them are those of the Dutch family Leyden. The carved door and the bird painting by de Koninck over the fireplace are of particular interest.

The roof timbers are the 14th century originals and are thought to have once been a ship's timbers.

Brussels tapestry woven by Jan Cobus

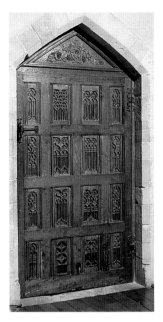

The carved door

THE BEER CELLAR

After returning through the Long Drawing Room you descend the Grand Staircase and turn left into the outer porch. From here a staircase leads down to the cellars. During the 19th and early 20th centuries, beer was brewed on the premises in what is now the outside tearoom. It was piped under the inner courtyard to the cellar. The large casks hold 600 gallons and the small ones 450.

other side by a row of ancient yews which were once clipped into the shape of elephants but which during the war years suffered an inevitable neglect and grew beyond redemption of the original topiary design. It is well worth walking to the end of the Bowling Alley to obtain fine views of the Castle.

Below the Alley is a long rectangular swimming pool, now a lily pond.

THE GARDEN

The meadows surrounding the Castle could be flooded at will to make life more difficult for any potential adversary. The ditches are locally called Rheens, a word derived from the river Rhine.

The late Captain Berkeley simplified the terraces into grass walks with a narrow border of low plants and some choice shrubs and climbers against the walls. The Bowling Alley is flanked on one side by an immensely high wall and on the

Across the meadows the visitor can see the kennels and stables of the Berkeley Hunt and beyond on the high ground, the Deer Park with its herds of red and fallow deer.

BUTTERFLY FARM

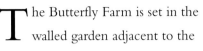

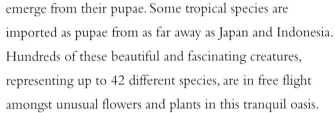

The Butterfly Farm is set in the walled garden adjacent to the car park. Exotic and British butterflies are flying here and you may see them emerge from their pupae. Some tropical species are imported as pupae from as far away as Japan and Indonesia. Hundreds of these beautiful and fascinating creatures, representing up to 42 different species, are in free flight amongst unusual flowers and plants in this tranquil oasis.

The Plant Centre, stocked with indoor and outdoor varieties is located here.

SPETCHLEY PARK

The Worcestershire home of Mr. and Mrs. R.J.G. Berkeley. This beautiful garden, situated two miles east of Worcester on the A422, extends over 25 acres. It is a plantsman's delight, containing many rare and unusual trees, shrubs and plants. Close by is the Deer Park, with its herds of red and fallow deer. Refreshments are obtainable in the garden. The house is not open to visitors.

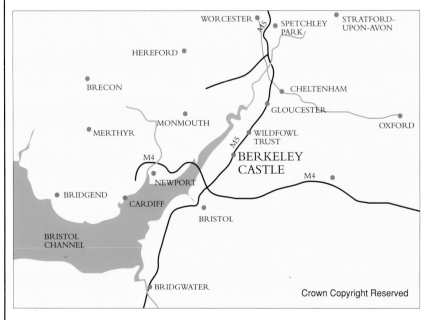

For information concerning opening times and admission charges, write to:
The Agent, Spetchley Park Garden, Spetchley, Worcester WR5 1RS.
Telephone 01905-345213/345224.

THE BERKELEY FAMILY

The history of the Berkeley Manor goes back to the reign of Edward the Confessor (1042-1066) when it was held by Earl Godwin, father of King Harold who fell at the battle of Senlac. Earl Godwin may possibly have had some small dwelling on the site of the present Castle; it seems probable, but in the absence of documentary evidence we cannot be sure. After the Conquest, Godwin having been despoiled of his possessions, Berkeley was handed over by William the Conqueror together with Bristol, Hereford, Gloucester and Chepstow to William FitzOsbern, Earl of Hereford and hereditary Steward of Normandy (*d.* 1071), to hold as the western defences of the new kingdom against the Welsh Marches across the Severn.

This FitzOsbern, recognising the strategic value of a site on a dominating hill, very naturally strengthened its position by building up the existing mound, surrounding it by a ditch, and setting a stout wooden stockade around the top. Defence was very primitive in those days, and FitzOsbern's *castellulum* or little castle probably resembled something we should now think of as 'native' in terms of an African or Indian stronghold. It certainly bore no resemblance to Berkeley Castle as we see it today; but it does mean that it formed the foundation of the

5th Earl of Berkeley by Pompeo Batoni

present Keep, and thus must be regarded as the original parent of the existing structure.

All other trace of FitzOsbern's elementary little fortress has disappeared. It seems likely that it was demolished in 1088, when there was rebellious trouble in the Vale of Berkeley. But so important a site could not be allowed to fall into desuetude, and we may fairly presume that FitzOsbern's representative or provost, Roger, calling himself Roger de Berkeley, was charged with supervising a new construction. What we know for certain is that three successive Rogers held the fief from the King, and that Roger II entertained Henry I at Easter 1121, which means that there must have been at least some kind of crude lodging for the King's reception, and that Roger III was in occupation during the reign of Stephen until 1153.

This third Roger was then evicted by Stephen's rival Henry of Anjou (subsequently Henry II) and Berkeley was granted by Henry to Robert FitzHarding, a wealthy merchant and provost of Bristol who had financially assisted Henry in his war against Stephen. The name of Robert FitzHarding should be noted, as he is the forebear of the family which holds Berkeley in its possession until the present day. The antiquity of the family goes back even further, for Robert FitzHarding himself was grandson to a certain Abnod or Eadnoth, staller of horse-thane to Edward the Confessor.

There are few families left in England with the proud boast of an authenticated Anglo-Saxon descent.

It may also be noted in passing that Robert FitzHarding was evidently a man of peace rather than of war, as he founded St. Augustine's Abbey in Bristol, and retired there as a Canon, until his death in 1170.

A brief account of Robert FitzHarding's successors may here not come amiss.

The history of the family may easily turn into a mere list of names and dates, becoming more and more meaningless to us as it recedes further and further back. The only hope of getting an overall picture is to think of the outstanding hereditary characteristics re-appearing from generation to generation in its members. Thus we shall find the early Berkeleys, descendants of that man of peace, Robert FitzHarding, dubbed with nicknames showing them as men gentle rather than coarse, pugnacious, or boorish. Of course they fought. They had to. It was a turbulent age in English history, when feudal lords on the Welsh border could scarcely be expected to live a quiet domestic life on their estates. But if we consider that they were respectively called Make-peace, and The Wise, and The Magnanimous, and The Magnificent, and (we are sorry to say) The Waste-all, we shall get the impression of surprisingly civilised people emerging in uncivilised centuries.

30

Besides, the early Berkeleys seem always to have been on the right side in the contemporary quarrels. They opposed King John, and supported Simon de Montfort. They disapproved of the weak Edward II and his favourites, yet they did not ill-treat Edward II when he came into their hands as a prisoner.

Robert FitzHarding's son Maurice, 2nd Lord Berkeley (*d*. 1190) known as Make-peace because of his diplomatically astute marriage with the daughter of the former occupier Roger de Berkeley (in order to settle the inheritance), has left his mark on the Castle by adding a tower or forebuilding opposite the Keep, also the curtain walls of the inner and outer courtyards. He evidently made the Castle his home, in a sense that his predecessors had never done. His son Robert II temporarily lost possession of his property as a result of siding with the barons at Runnymede when King John was compelled to sign Magna Carta; it was restored to the Berkeleys in the following reign (Henry III) in 1223.

Maurice II (*d*. 1281) took arms with Simon de Montfort against Henry III: his son Thomas, known as the Wise and described as 'a wise and provident man', stood high in the favour of Edward I, took part in Edward's campaigns; fought at Bannockburn when he was already seventy; was captured by the Scots and released on payment of ransom. From his carefully-kept accounts we learn, amongst other details, that he was followed by two hundred attendants and paid 3d a day to his squire who likewise received a horse and two suits of clothes annually.

This Thomas was the first of his family to be summoned by writ to Parliament, and thus should be considered as the first Lord Berkeley *de jure*, his predecessors having enjoyed that title only by tenure. He died in 1321.

His son Maurice III, the Magnanimous, seems to have inherited his father's qualities, and became Seneschal of Aquitaine. He got into trouble however for opposing Edward II and for raiding the estates of Edward's favourite, Hugh le Despenser, and died imprisoned in Wallingford Castle, 1326. This brings us to his son Thomas III, Lord of Berkeley when the unfortunate Edward II was brought there as a prisoner in April 1327.

We may quickly pass over the successive generations down to the present day. Thomas III (*d*. 1361) was forgiven by Edward III for any part he may have played in the downfall and murder of Edward II, and rose to some eminence in military commands, also in diplomatic missions to Pope Innocent VI at Avignon. His grandson Thomas IV, the Magnificent, (*d*. 1417) entertained Richard II at Berkeley. Thomas IV, dying

without a son, the Castle then passed to a nephew, James (*d*. 1463) and became the subject of much dispute between various claimants. These family quarrels are not of much interest to us today, unless we are deeply absorbed in the details of medieval Gloucestershire chronicles. But William, the Waste-all, must be mentioned since he bartered the Castle and Estates with Henry VII in exchange for numerous titles and the inheritance remained a Royal Castle until the death of Edward VI. Let us skip over Maurice V and Maurice VI and even over Thomas V who, dispossessed of his Castle, pursued the life of a country squire, "living a kind of Grazier's life, having his flocks summering in one place and wintering in other places, as he observed the fields and pastures to be sound and could bargain best cheap".

Then comes his grandson Henry, who at the age of nineteen regained possession of his Castle on the death of King Edward VI, 1553. We know a lot about this Henry, who sounds an attractive and typically English character, flying his own falcons and hunting his own hounds "inferior to no man's through great choice of whelps", playing bowls with his 'long and slender and lady-like hand' and taking great pleasure in company.

This cheerful and sociable young man died in 1613, aged eighty or thereabouts, having, we hope, enjoyed his life as Lord of Berkeley, and being succeeded by his grandson George. George came in for the troubled period of Charles I and the Civil War, when Berkeley was captured by the Parliamentary forces after a siege of three days. They did not do as much damage as might have been expected, and George was left with his home more or less intact except for a breach in the wall of the Keep, a great square bite out of the massive wall, which still remains as a vivid evidence of the continuity of our English history in the stones of our ancestral houses.

George, described as a man of 'singular bounty and affability' was succeeded by his son, another George, who enjoyed the favour of King Charles II, by whom he was made Earl of Berkeley in 1679. We may now pass on to Frederick Augustus, the 5th Earl, on whose death in 1810 some trouble arose over a question of legitimacy involving the succession to the title, and culminated in the notorious Berkeley Peerage Case, which was brought before the House of Lords in 1811. To put it briefly, the 5th Earl had fallen in love with a certain Mary Cole, daughter of a Gloucestershire tradesman, and the whole dispute hinged on whether a secret marriage had taken place, as the Earl alleged, in 1785, some ten or twelve years earlier than the official marriage in 1796. Were the older sons legitimate or not, or must they give way to their younger brothers, born after the official marriage? The case was decided against them, so William the eldest son of the doubtful marriage couldn't inherit the title. He did, however, inherit the Castle, and by way of compensation mainly because of his political influence, was created Lord FitzHardinge in his own right in 1841, the earldom of Berkeley passing to the eldest legitimate son and subsequently by collateral branches of the family to the sixth, seventh and eighth Earls of Berkeley.

Meanwhile, the title of Lord FitzHardinge continued with the *de facto* owners of the Castle, Maurice the next brother of William, and his sons Francis William and Charles. Charles dying without children in 1916, the Castle and the Berkeley earldom became re-united in tail male in the person of the eighth Earl of Berkeley, a distinguished scientist and Fellow of the Royal Society. He died in 1942.

Both titles are now extinct, but it is agreeable to be able to record that the present owner, Mr. R.J.G. Berkeley, is a lineal descendant in the twenty-fourth generation of old Robert FitzHarding (to whom the Castle was granted in 1153 by Henry II) that man of peace, whose name stands at the beginning of this short survey of one of our oldest families.

We have tried to build up a picture of an ancient family with its great possessions and all the tribulations that attend on such families for one reason or another throughout the centuries of our English history. We have tried to emphasise that the lords of Berkeley were on the whole peace-loving men, fond of their Castle, and builders of their Castle, for after all, we must never forget that successive lords of Berkeley added and added to their old fortress until they had turned it into the astonishing pile we see today.

There is one aspect of the Berkeleys which we have perhaps omitted to emphasise. Feudal lords they might be, involved in the political and regional struggles of their own days, but essentially we see them as country squires, looking after their estates and deeply concerned with their hounds and horses. The fifth Earl hunted his hounds from Berkeley to Charing Cross. The season started at Berkeley; the whole establishment was then moved to Nettlebed in Oxfordshire for a month, and then on to Gerrards Cross to hunt the London country and then in stages back to Berkeley where the season ended.

The Berkeley Hounds by Lionel Edwards

This was considered a too complicated business, so a part of the pack together with the famous huntsman Oldacre (so often painted by Ben Marshall) were left behind to hunt the "London country". They have remained ever since and until 1970 called themselves the Old Berkeley; they are now the Vale of Aylesbury and they still retain the yellow coats. The Berkeley Hunt to this day differs from other Hunts, in that its Hunt servants wear a yellow coat, not a red coat.

It fits in very neatly with our conception of a race of English aristocrats, half-conventional and half-eccentric without the slightest idea that they were behaving eccentrically at all.

Although the family and the Castle's contents are fascinating, it is the exterior that is surely the most impressive. The walls have been compared to the colour of pot-pourri, dried rose-petals mixed with the grey of lavender, and that is really an almost exact description, for anyone who has the eye to see it. In certain lights, especially in those odd effects of light that come at sunset, the Castle turns almost purple, with the red valerian sprouting out of the walls to enhance the strange hues of the stone. That is the hour to see it at its best, looking up from the meadows it seems like a natural cliff, growing with its bastions and abutments in geological formation following the contours of the escarpment. It is hard to realise that this is a man-made stronghold, rugged indeed, but still the home of men whose ancestors built it.

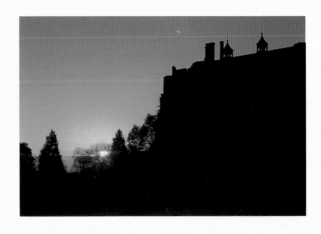